MY FIRS
EASTER
HIGH CONTRAST BABY BOOK

THIS BOOK BELONGS TO:

____

____

Happy
Easter

GUIDANCES

HOW OFTEN SHOULD YOU VIEV THE BOOKS?

DO IT EVERY DAY. SHOW YOUR CHILD FOR AT LEAST A FEW MINUTES EVERY DAY. "WATCH AS MUCH AS YOU CAN."

HOW LONG SHOULD BABIES LOOK AT BLACK AND WHITE CARDS?

LET YOUR CHILD FOCUS ON THE PICTURE FOR A SHORT TIME, NO LONGER THAN 30 SECONDS AT A TIME.

MOTOR DEVELOPMENT - HAND-EYE?

ENCOURAGE YOUR BABY TO REACH FOR THE CARD AND EXAMINE IT WITH THEIR HANDS.

HO-HO-HO!

ENJOY THE GIFT INSIDE

https://bit.ly/**********

THE GIFT IN PAGE 26

HO-HO-HO!

HERE IS YOUR GIFT:

https://bit.ly/4f4Y0oW

TAP THIS LINK IN THE BROWSER AND ENJOY!
IF YOU LOVED THE BOOK AND THE GIFT GIVE US

★★★★★

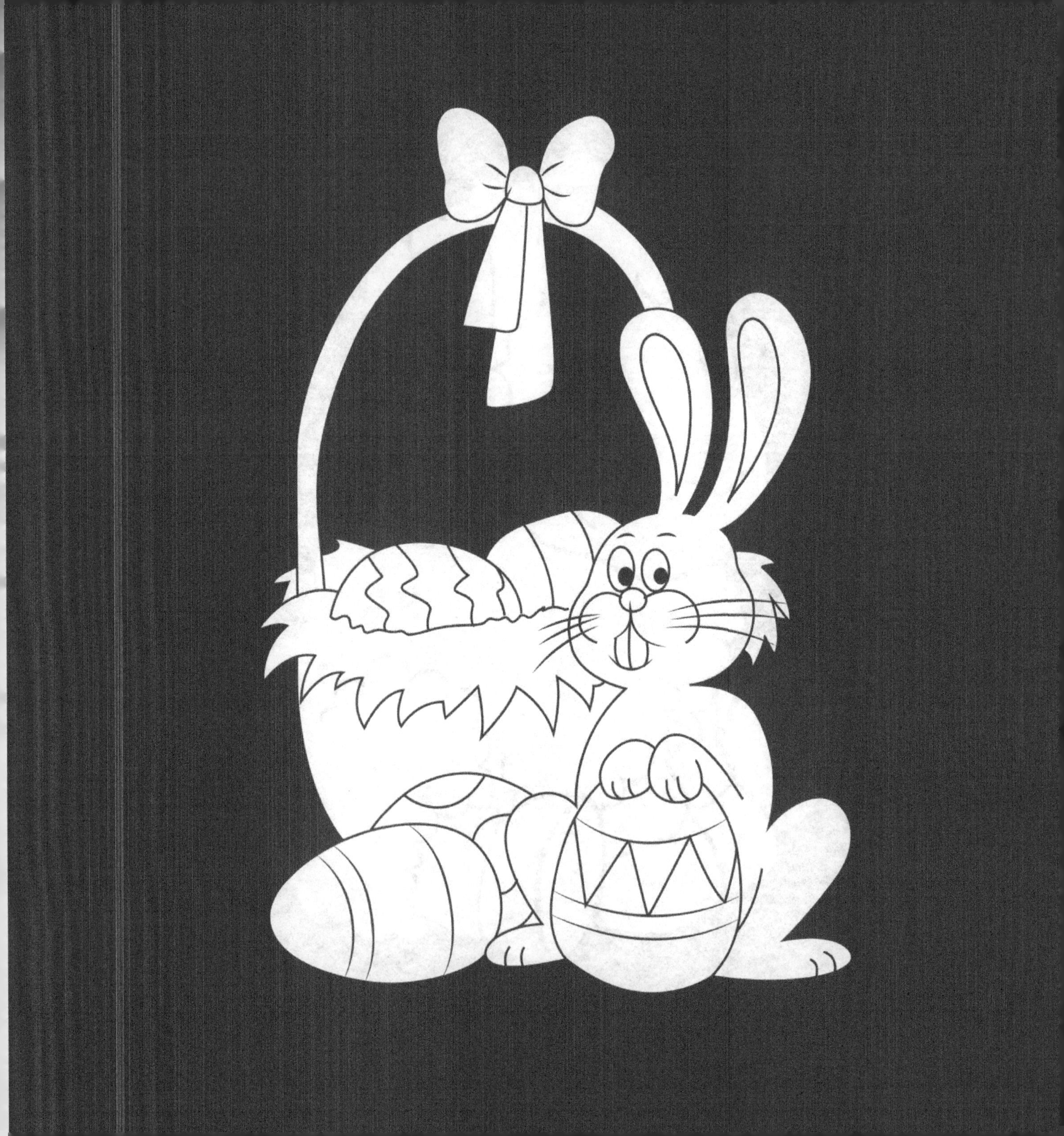

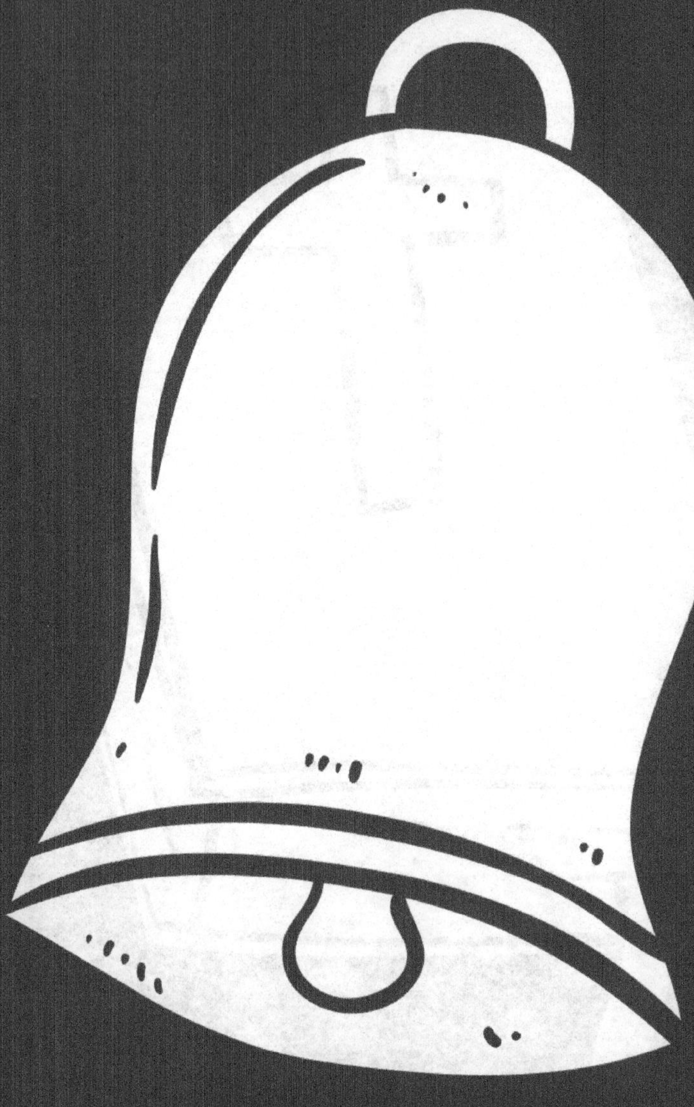

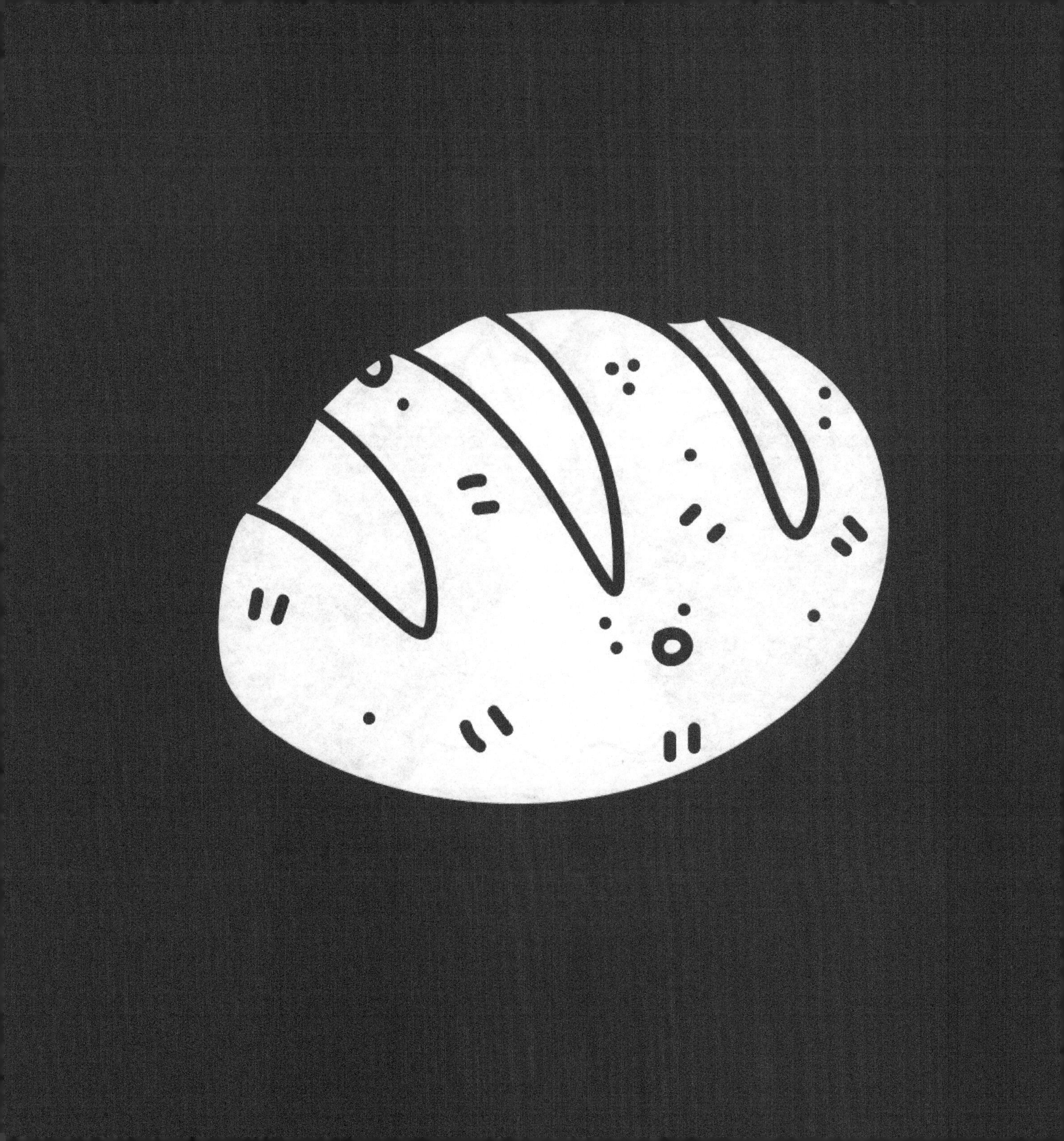

Happy
Easter

Made in the USA
Monee, IL
27 March 2025

14758673R00059